God's Angels, Our Friends

Stories & Activities about Angels
for Grades 3 to 6

Cover Image: "Snowflake" by Ted DeGrazia
Cover image courtesy of the DeGrazia Foundation in Tucson, Arizona, USA.

Imprimatur:
Most Rev. Gerald F. Kicanas, Bishop of Tucson

The Nihil Obstat and the Imprimatur are a declaration that a book is considered free from doctrinal or moral error. It is not implied that those who have granted the Nihil Obstat and Imprimatur agree with the contents, opinions or statements expressed.

Scripture texts in this work are taken from the *New Revised Standard Version Bible: Catholic Edition*, © 1989, 1993, Division of Christian Education of the National Council of the Churches of Christ in the United States of America. Used by permission. All rights reserved.

THE BOOK TEAM

- Ernie Nedder, Publisher
- Kathy Nedder, CFO
- Sister Mary Kathleen Glavich, SND, Author and Illustrator
- Rev. Thomas M. Santa, CSsR, Theological Editor
- Kate Harrison, Editor
- Lone Quail Media, Design Services
        Jolene Campbell, Designer

Additional copies of this publication may be purchased by sending check or money order for $15 plus $5 postage and handling to: Theological Book Service, P.O. Box 509, Barnhart, MO 63012. Or call toll free 1-888-247-3023. Fax: 1-800-325-9526. E-mail: sales@fillorders.com. Be sure to check our Web site for a list of other products: www.nedderpublishing.com.

Order # 42-0
8 1/2 x 11

Individual copies: $15.
Multiple copy discounts available.

ISBN: 1-893757-42-0

Table of Contents

Introduction for Teachers and Parents

Sister Anne, who is in her eighties, keeps a picture of a guardian angel on the wall by her bed. She explains, "One day when I was a little girl, I was about to jump off the school bus as usual, but I felt an arm holding me back. Suddenly out of nowhere a car zoomed by the bus. If I had not been stopped, I would have been injured or killed. Strangely, no one was behind me on the bus stairwell. I believe that my guardian angel was taking care of me that day, and I've had a devotion to him ever since."

Some people like Sister Anne believe in angels. Some don't. "Nonbelievers" view angels as merely a myth borrowed from unenlightened cultures. To them, archangels make impressive statues, and cherubs make whimsical art, but they are not real or necessary. These people reason that God is present to us, so why do we need angels? *The Catechism of the Catholic Church* differs. It states, "The existence of the spiritual, non-corporeal beings that Sacred Scripture usually calls 'angels' is a truth of faith." (#328)

The Catholic Church has always taught that there are majestic beings in heaven who are pure spirits created by God. They praise and serve God, and some of them act as God's messengers. What's more, God assigns each human being one angel as a guide and protector on the journey to heaven. In fact, St. Augustine taught that there is a guardian angel assigned to every city, every building, every visible thing!

Both the Scripture writers and tradition assume that angels exist. The Bible reveals the names of some of the seven archangels: Michael, Gabriel and Raphael. In the Gospels Jesus speaks of angels. He says, "Take care that you do not despise one of these little ones; for, I tell you, in heaven their angels continually see the face of my Father in heaven." (Matthew 18:10) Saints have prayed to angels and have been favored by visits and conversations with angels. Many people can relate stories like Sister Anne's. Some even claim that when they forget to set their alarm, their guardian angel wakes them up on time! No wonder angels are popular in our culture today.

Teaching Children about Angels

When we teach our children about the angels, we share with them a beautiful facet of our faith. Angels are already engaged in our intended destiny: glorifying God in heaven. Most strikingly, angels are a powerful expression of God's tender, loving care for each one of us. They are a personification of this characteristic of God. Children find it consoling and helpful to know that they have an invisible friend constantly at their side.

This activity book introduces children to the angels. It helps them to understand the angels' role in creation, their presence in Scripture and their interaction with us. In the process the children learn prayers to the angels, read stories about their appearances and most importantly come to appreciate even more our heavenly Father's love for us.

With the assistance of angels on earth, may we and our children someday join their choirs in heaven singing "Holy, holy, holy!" to our Creator.

Meet God's Angels

† Angel Facts

Finish the facts. Unscramble the letters in ( ) and write the word on the line.

Origin   Angels are created by (odG) _____

Make-up   Angels are pure spirits like God. They have no (oydb) _____.
Angels are invisible.

Powers   Angels can (knhit) _____, (oshoec) _____ and love.
They are smarter, more powerful and greater than human beings.

Job   Angels (isepar) _____ God and act as God's agents.

Home   Angels live in (venahe) _____. They are saints.

† Name Game

What does the word *angel* mean?
Write the letter of the alphabet that comes before the given one to find out.

__ __ __ __ __ __ __ __ __

N   F   T   T   F   O   H   F   S

† Levels of Creation

Number God's creations from least (1) to greatest (4).

What Angels Look Like

Although angels are invisible, artists draw them with  . They give them white

and put over their to show that angels are holy and reflect

God's glory. Sometimes artists draw angels with to show that they move quickly. In

the Bible the prophet Isaiah had a vision of angels with **6** . When angels appear to

people they may take on a human body. Sometimes in art angels are shown as chubby

. These little angels are called cherubs.

† Angel Art
In the frame draw an angel as you imagine one.

Angels Give Glory to God

Angels do what we were created to do. They praise God forever. The prophet Isaiah saw angels in heaven praising God. They sang: "Holy, holy, holy is the LORD of hosts! All the earth is filled with his glory!" (Isaiah 6:3)
Hosts means very many, an army.

Does the angels' song sound familiar? At Mass we sing this song. We join the hosts of angels praising God.

What is your favorite hymn?

_____

† **Praise God!**

In each note write or draw something you praise God for.
Color and decorate the "Holy, Holy" to make it beautiful.

Angels as Messengers

Genesis 18:1–15; 22:1–18

In the Bible God often sends angels with messages for people. God sent angels to the first believers, Abraham and Sarah. Three mysterious visitors (God and two angels) told them that although they were old, they would have a son, Isaac. Later God tested Abraham's faith.

In those days people thought that they pleased their gods by destroying crops, animals and even human beings in their honor. These offerings are called sacrifices. One day God told Abraham to sacrifice his son Isaac. This puzzled Abraham because God had told him he would have as many descendants as the stars. Nevertheless, he took Isaac up a mountain and built an altar. Then he tied up his son and laid him on the altar. Just as Abraham took out his knife, an angel called his name and told him not to touch Isaac. Abraham found a ram in the bushes to sacrifice instead.

† No Human Sacrifice

In the picture find and circle a ram, a knife, an angel and seven stars. Color the stones with 1 in them to read Abraham's greatest virtue.

Your Guardian Angel

On the day you were born, God put a special angel in charge of you. This guardian angel, a heavenly bodyguard, is with you at all times. Your angel is a sign of how much God loves and cares for you. Jesus said that our angels always look on our heavenly Father's face. (Matthew 18:10) Our angels help us to live as God's children, pray for us and take our prayers to heaven. Some people believe that a guardian angel also watches over each parish, city and nation.

What name would you like to give your guardian angel?

_____

† Angel Duties

In the word search puzzle find and circle the words in the Word Box that tell what your guardian angel does for you. The words are horizontal, vertical and diagonal.

Word Box

Care	Guard
Guide	Pray
Protect	Direct
Love	Enlighten
Inspire	Watch

```
G  L  O  V  E  E  I  S  T  G  M
C  U  N  R  J  W  V  I  Q  U  D
D  E  A  H  G  A  R  X  E  I  W
I  C  P  R  O  T  E  C  T  D  F
R  O  S  C  D  C  Y  U  B  E  Y
E  N  L  I  G  H  T  E  N  A  W
C  N  O  E  S  R  Y  P  R  L  X
T  E  H  W  I  N  S  P  I  R  E
```

The Feast of the Guardian Angels is October 2.

You could celebrate your angel this day by going to Mass or by saying a special prayer.

QUOTATION
Experience the presence of the angels next to you and allow yourselves to be guided by them.
—Pope John Paul II

Guardian Angel: Guide and Protector

Another name for angels is watchers because they watch over us. Our guardian angels protect us from bodily harm. They also steer us away from things that endanger our spiritual life.

† Angel Hints

Put a ◯ (halo) before each action that your guardian angel might urge you to do.
Put an ✗ before things your angel would tell you not to do.

Do what my mother says	Do my homework well
Eat junk food	Steal a little
Share my things	Clean my room
Say my morning prayers	Talk about others' faults
Talk about another's faults	Pout when I don't get my way
Take dares that risk my life	Harm other children
Participate in Sunday Mass	Use bad words
Tell lies	Visit an elderly or sick person
Be kind to someone others avoid	Give someone a gift
Help my mom or dad	Thank God for good things

QUOTATION
He [our guardian angel] is our most sincere and faithful friend even when we sadden him with our bad behavior.
— St. Pio of Pietrelcino

† Angel Interview
Ask several people if they think they were ever helped or saved by an angel.

† Angels on the Internet
Learn more about angels from the Internet. Type "angels" into the search engine.

Guardian Angel Prayers

Memorize one of the prayers below and pray it every night before you go to bed.
Hint: Keep a copy of the prayer near your bed until you know it by heart.

Prayer to the Guardian Angel

Angel sent by God to guide me,
Be my light and walk beside me;
Be my guardian and protect me;
On the paths of life direct me.
Amen.

† † † † † † † † † † †

Traditional Prayer

Angel of God, my guardian dear,
To whom God's love commits* me here,
Ever this day be at my side
To light and to guard to rule and to guide.
Amen.

* *Commits* means entrusts.

† 911 Prayers
When you are in danger or in a predicament, call on your guardian angel for help.
Write a prayer here to your guardian angel:

_____

_____

_____

_____

_____

Guardian Angel Board Game

† Put a small object at Start. Toss a coin. If it lands on heads go forward two spaces. If it lands on tails, go forward one space. Keep track of how many tosses it takes you to get to heaven. Try to beat your own record or play with a friend.

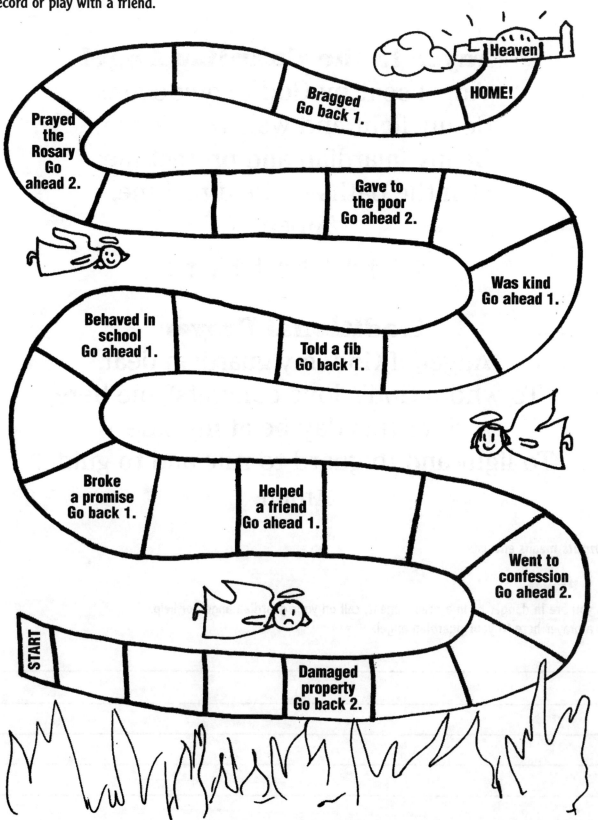

Heaven

HOME!

Bragged
Go back 1.

Prayed
the
Rosary
Go
ahead 2.

Gave to
the poor
Go ahead 2.

Was kind
Go ahead 1.

Behaved in
school
Go ahead 1.

Told a fib
Go back 1.

Broke
a promise
Go back 1.

Helped
a friend
Go ahead 1.

Went to
confession
Go ahead 2.

START

Damaged
property
Go back 2.

Choirs of Angels

The Bible mentions angels 222 times and refers to several kinds. In the 4th century nine choirs (groups) of angels were named. Here they are from greatest to least:

1	Seraphim	4	Dominations	7	Principalities
2	Cherubim	5	Virtues	8	Archangels
3	Thrones	6	Powers	9	Angels

Cherubim and seraphim guard God's throne. In the prophet Isaiah's vision, angels near God's throne were seraphim with six wings. In the book of Genesis after the Fall of Adam and Eve, God had the cherubim guard the path to the tree of life in Eden. (Genesis 3:24) Cherubim are mighty angels — not at all like the cherubs that are named for them. We know the names of some of the archangels. Our guardian angels belong to the last choir.

Mary, the Mother of God and our heavenly mother, is Queen of Angels.

† Name the Archangels
Write the letters above all the 1s in order on the lines. Do the same for the 2s and 3s and you will see the names of the three popular archangels.

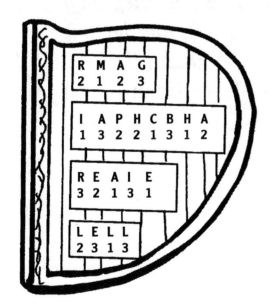

1s __ __ __ __ __ __ __

2s __ __ __ __ __ __ __

3s __ __ __ __ __ __

† Angel Count
How many angels do you think there are?

_____

(Look up Revelation 5:11 in
the last book in the Bible, to see the answer.)

QUOTATION
You might wish to understand these angels as the eyes or the ears or the hands or the feet of God.
— St. Hilary

Angel History
Revelation 12:7–9

The Book of Revelation and tradition tell about a cosmic war story. Before time began, the most brilliant angel was Lucifer, whose name means "light." Lucifer rebelled against God. He led other angels who also rebelled. A great battle took place between the forces of Lucifer and the angels who were faithful to God. The good angels, led by the Archangel Michael, were victorious.

The bad angels were cast into hell and are now known as devils, demons or Satan. Jesus once said, "I watched Satan fall from heaven like a flash of lightning." (Luke 10:18) When we human beings turned against God, we had a second chance. The bad angels didn't because they are more intelligent than human beings.

Devils do not want us to take their places in heaven praising God, their enemy. They tempt us to sin so that we end up like them. In art, devils are red because they live in fire. They are drawn with horns and a tail because Satan appears as a dragon in the Book of Revelation.

† Life and Death
Remove "d" from *devil*: _____
Write *evil* backwards: _____
The devil brings the opposite of life — eternal death. Jesus conquers evil.

† Heavenly Flag
Design a flag that Michael and the good angels might have carried into battle.

QUOTATION
I came that they may have life, and have it abundantly.
— Jesus (John 10:10)

St. Michael: God's Fighter

Daniel 10:21

We celebrate St. Michael the Archangel's feast on September 29. This day is also known as Michaelmas Day. If your name is Michael or Michelle, this is your nameday!

† Coded Info

Use the code here to complete the information about St. Michael.

A	B	C	D	E	F	G	H	I	J	K	L	M	N	O	P	Q	R	S	T	U	V	W	X	Y	Z
✡	✚	■	♣	✥	✦	✧	★	☆	☉	✫	✩	●	✪	✭	☆	✴	✎	✶	✵	✶✶	□	✹	✺	

St. Michael is called _____ in the Bible. He led the angels to victory
☆ ✵ ☆ ★ ■ ♣

against _____. Michael means "_____ _____ _____ _____?"
✎ ✡ ✵ ☆ ★   ✶ ★ ✵   ☆ ✎   ★ ☆ ★ ♣   ✧ ★ ■

We think this was angels' battle cry. In art St. Michael is usually a young man wearing

_____ and pointing a _____ at Satan, who lies at his feet.
✡ ✵ ● ★ ✵   ✎ ✶ ★ ✵ ♣

You might pray to St. Michael in times of _____.
✶ ♣ ● ☆ ✶ ✡ ✶ ☆ ★ ★

It's said that St. Michael fights for people's salvation especially at the hour of their death.

Also, he is thought to _____ the dead into the next life and present them for
★ ♣ ✡ ♣

judgment then and at the end of the world. This is why sometimes he is shown holding

_____ or a book of life. St. Michael was the protector of the Israelites and
✎ ■ ✡ ★ ♣ ✎

is now patron of the _____ Church. He is also patron of
■ ✡ ✵ ★ ★ ★ ☆ ■

_____, policemen, grocers, radiologists, sailors, the sick and dying,
✎ ★ ★ ♣ ☆ ♣ ✺ ✎

and the countries of England, Germany, Papua New Guinea and the Solomon Islands.

Prayer to St. Michael the Archangel

During a plague in Rome in the year 590 A.D. Pope St. Gregory the Great led a procession as an act of penance. St. Michael appeared to him and indicated that the plague would end. Today there is a large statue of St. Michael at the top of the Castel Sant' Angelo in Rome.

In the 15th century St. Joan of Arc said that St. Michael, along with St. Catherine and St. Margaret, appeared to her and told her to lead the French army. She obeyed and won a battle at Orleans against England on the feast of St. Michael!

Here is a good prayer to pray when bad things happen in the world or when you are tempted. You might memorize it.

Saint Michael the Archangel,
defend us in battle.
Be our protection against
the wickedness and snares of the devil.
May God rebuke him, we humbly pray.
And you, Prince of the heavenly host,
by the power of God,
thrust into hell Satan
and the other evil spirits
who prowl about the world
seeking the ruin of souls. Amen.

Dictionary

Snares – traps
Rebuke – force back

Host – army of angels
Ruin of souls – eternal death in hell

† Know Your Church

St. Michael is patron of the Church. Can you answer these questions about the Church?

Who is the Pope, its visible head? _____

Where is the Church's headquarters? _____

Who is the founder of the Church? _____

When was it founded? _____

Who is the bishop of your diocese? _____

Who is your pastor? _____

St. Gabriel: God's Messenger

The Church celebrates St. Gabriel the Archangel's feastday on September 29. In the Bible Gabriel was sent by God to three people with messages:

PEOPLE	MESSAGE
Daniel, the prophet	The angel told him the meaning of his visions. (Daniel 8:15–26; 9:20–27)
Zechariah, father of John the Baptist	He and his wife, Elizabeth, would have a son to be named John. (Luke 1:5–25)
Mary, Mother of God	God chose her to be the mother of the Savior. Gabriel came as a young man and greeted Mary, "Hail, Mary, full of grace. The Lord is with you." (Luke 1:26–38)

It is a good idea to pray to St. Gabriel when you want to know and do God's will. He is the patron of postal services, telephone, telegraph and television workers. His name means "Strength of God."

† Earthshaking News

Read the story of the Annunciation in Luke 1:26–38. Thank God for becoming man and thank Mary for saying yes.

† Hear Ye! Hear Ye!

In each row find and put an X on the trumpet that is different. Then in order on the lines write the words under the similar trumpets to see Gabriel's message.

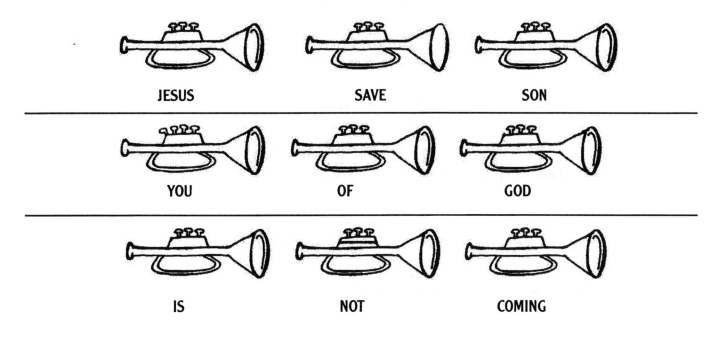

JESUS   SAVE   SON

YOU   OF   GOD

IS   NOT   COMING

The Angelus

When you pray the Hail Mary, you echo Gabriel's words to Mary in the first sentence. Three Hail Marys are part of a prayer in honor of the day Gabriel appeared to Mary. This prayer is called the Angelus because of its opening words. *Angelus* is Latin for "angel." The Church used to ring bells to remind people to pray the Angelus morning, noon and night. Some bells are engraved "Gabriel." At noon on Sundays the Pope leads the Angelus for people gathered in St. Peter's Square in Rome. Learn the Angelus and pray it.

† Artwork

Decorate around the Angelus. You might draw a lily or rose for Mary, an M for her, wings for Gabriel, a manger, a cross and a dove for the Holy Spirit.

The angel of the Lord declared unto Mary.
And she conceived by the Holy Spirit.

Hail Mary, full of grace, the Lord is with you.
Blessed are you among women and blessed is the fruit of your womb, Jesus.
Holy Mary, Mother of God, pray for us sinners now and at the hour of our death. Amen.

Behold the handmaid of the Lord.
Be it done unto me according to your word.

Hail Mary....

And the Word was made flesh.
And dwelt among us.

Hail Mary....

Pray for us, O Holy Mother of God.
That we may be made worthy of the promises of Christ.

Let us pray.
Pour forth, we beseech you, O Lord, your grace into our hearts; that, we to whom the Incarnation of Christ, your Son, was made known by the message of an angel, may by his passion and cross, be brought to the glory of his resurrection.
Through the same Christ our Lord. Amen.

St. Raphael: God's Healer

Here are some facts about St. Raphael.
- St. Raphael is one of the seven archangels.
- His feastday is September 29, which he shares with St. Michael and St. Gabriel.
- The name Raphael means "God has healed."
- St. Raphael is the patron of travelers, young people leaving home, the blind, nurses, physicians and lovers.

† The Book of Tobit

Raphael received his name and roles because of his actions in the Bible's Book of Tobit. Read the following story about St. Raphael, Tobit and Tobit's son, Tobias.

A man named Tobit was good and kind.
But one sad day he woke up blind.
He'd left some money with a friend far away
So he called for his son without delay

"Tobias," Tobit said, "you must live well.
You'll be rich if you do as I tell.
Go see my friend and get our money,
But find someone to guide you, Sonny."

Tobias found a man as soon as he went out
Who said he knew the way without a doubt.
The man was Raphael, an angel in disguise,
Sent by God to heal Tobit's eyes.

Tobias and Raphael walked 'til night.
Then washing his feet, Tobias had a fright.
A fish tried to swallow his foot in the river.
Said Raphael, "Catch it. Save its gall, heart and liver."

For days they walked. Then Raphael said,
"Tonight at Raguel's we'll sleep in a bed.
He's your kin and it's your right
To wed his daughter. Sarah's lovely and bright.

Sarah had wed seven times before.
Each groom had dropped dead to the floor.
This occurred on his wedding night
Because of a jealous demon's might.

Continued on page 16

† The Book of Tobit (continued)

Raphael told Tobias, "Chase the demon away.
Burn the liver and heart with incense. Pray."
Tobias obeyed. He and Sarah were married,
While Raguel dug a grave, for Tobias to be buried.

When morning came, Tobias was alive!
Because of Raphael he did survive.
What's more, he inherited Raguel's wealth,
Recovered Tobit's money and returned in health.

At home once more Tobias was told,
"I can give you something better than gold.
Smear fish gall on old Tobit's eyes
And you will have a pleasant surprise."

For Tobias now Raphael's word was law.
He did as he said, and Tobit saw!
When Tobit offered to pay what Raphael earned
Both father and son a great thing learned.

The man who traveled at Tobias's side
Who caught him a fish and a pretty bride
Who got him riches and cured his dad
Was none other than an angel of God!

He was Raphael, one of seven
Who stand before God's throne in heaven.
With Tobit, Tobias sang God's praises,
Had seven sons and lived for ages.

† Fishing

Connect the dots from 1 through 37 and from A through J and color the picture.

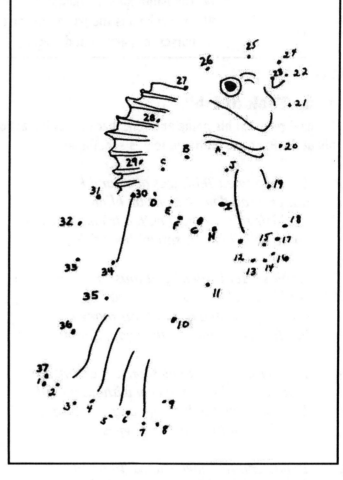

† God Heals Today

Cross out the first letter and every other one. Write the remaining letters on the lines to see how God may heal today.

O S T A I C U R O A E M L E S N R T C O D F A T X H Y E W A V N

B O Z I C N R T S I K N Q G P O C F D T X H Y E N S E I M C R K

__ __ __ __ __ __ __ __ __ __ __ __ __

__ __ __ __ __ __ __ __ __ __

__ __ __ __ __ __ __ __ __

Lot and the Angels

Genesis 19:1-29

The Bible tells a story about Abraham's nephew Lot. Lot, his wife, daughters and sons-in-law lived in the town of Sodom. One day two angels visited them with a message: Because Sodom was so wicked, it was going to be destroyed. The angels told Lot's family to flee. That night men tried to break into Lot's house, but angels made a blinding light so they couldn't find the door.

The next morning Lot's family did not leave right away. The angels had to take them by the hand and lead them out of the city. "Do not look back," the angels ordered. When Lot's family was safe, an earthquake hit Sodom. Fire and smoke covered it. Curious, Lot's wife looked back and turned into a pillar of salt! The Dead Sea in the Holy Land is full of salt and other chemicals that prevent life from growing. Nearby are strange rock formations. This could be the remains of Sodom.

† It Pays to Obey!

Lot's angels carry God's message, protect his family, advise them and lead them to safety. Your guardian angel helps you follow God's laws so that someday you will be safe in heaven. Go through the maze. At each road sign, unscramble the letters to spell what the Commandment(s) tells you to do.

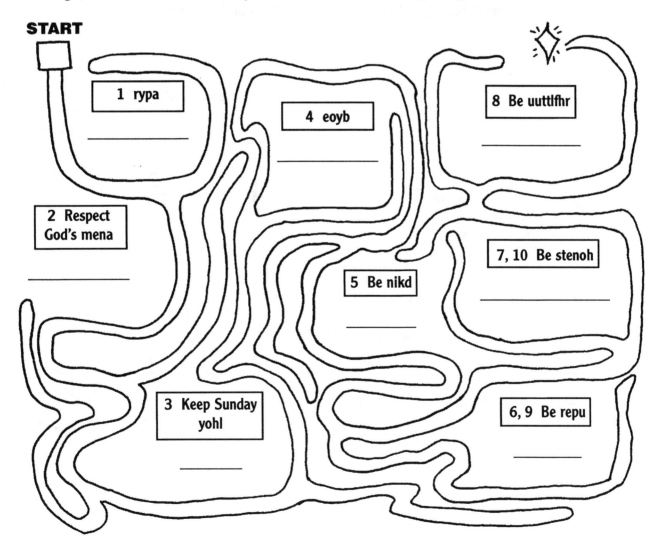

START

1 rypa

4 eoyb

8 Be uuttlfhr

2 Respect God's mena

7, 10 Be stenoh

5 Be nikd

3 Keep Sunday yohl

6, 9 Be repu

17

Hagar and the Angel

Genesis 16:1-16; 21:9-21

Hagar, from Egypt, was Sarah's maid. Because Sarah had no children, Abraham, Sarah's husband, was to have a child with Hagar, as was the custom. When Hagar became pregnant, she looked down on Sarah. Then Sarah was so mean to Hagar that she ran away. At a spring in the desert an angel told Hagar to return. He promised that she would have a son Ishmael and many descendants. Hagar went back.

After Hagar had Ishmael and Sarah had Isaac, Sarah feared that Ishmael would share Isaac's inheritance. She made Abraham send Hagar and Ishmael away. God told Abraham to do as Sarah said and promised that Ishmael would be a great nation. So Hagar was sent into the desert with some bread and water. When the water was gone, Hagar set Ishmael down to die. Hearing the boy's cries, God sent an angel. He told Hagar not to be afraid. God would make Ishmael a great nation. When Hagar opened her eyes, she saw a well. Ishmael grew up to be an excellent archer and married an Egyptian girl.

† Hidden Message

Because God loved Abraham, he had plans for both of his sons, Isaac and Ishmael. He said, "Ishmael will be a great nation." Starting at the arrow, trace the letters of this promise in the well.

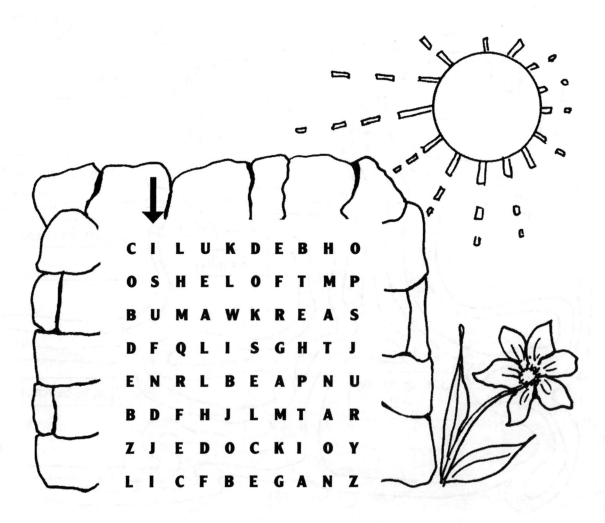

Jacob's Vision of Angels

Genesis 28:10–18

Jacob, Abraham's grandson, was on his way to find a wife. At sunset, he came to a shrine. He took a stone from it for a pillow and lay on the ground to sleep. During the night Jacob saw a stairway connecting earth to heaven. Angels were going up and down it. Suddenly God stood beside Jacob and renewed the promises he had made to Abraham. Jacob would have many descendants through whom the world would be blessed. God would give them the land Jacob was on. Also, God would protect Jacob. When Jacob awoke, he exclaimed that the shrine was a holy spot, the gateway to heaven. He poured oil on the stone and set it up as a memorial, a marker to always remember what happened there. He promised God one-tenth of all he received.

† Tithing

Tithing is giving God part of what you own. You can tithe by putting money in the basket at Mass. You can also offer God prayers and good deeds.

What will you give God this week? _____

† Your Holy Place

What is the name of the church where you meet God? _____

Where it have images of angels? _____

Draw the inside of your church below.

Moses and the Burning Bush

Exodus 3:1–22

At one time the Israelites were slaves in Egypt. One of them named Moses was tending his father-in-law's sheep. He took them to Mount Horeb. There Moses saw an angel of the Lord in fire flaming out of a bush. Strangely, the bush was not hurt. Then God called to Moses from the bush. He told Moses that he had chosen him to lead his people out of Egypt to a land flowing with milk and honey. Moses was to go to the Pharaoh, king of Egypt. God would be with him. God revealed his name to Moses as "I Am Who Am." With God's help, Moses led the Israelites to freedom, to the promised land.

† Your Call

Connect the dots to make flames around some things that God may call you to be.
If you think God calls you to be something not listed, write it here: _____

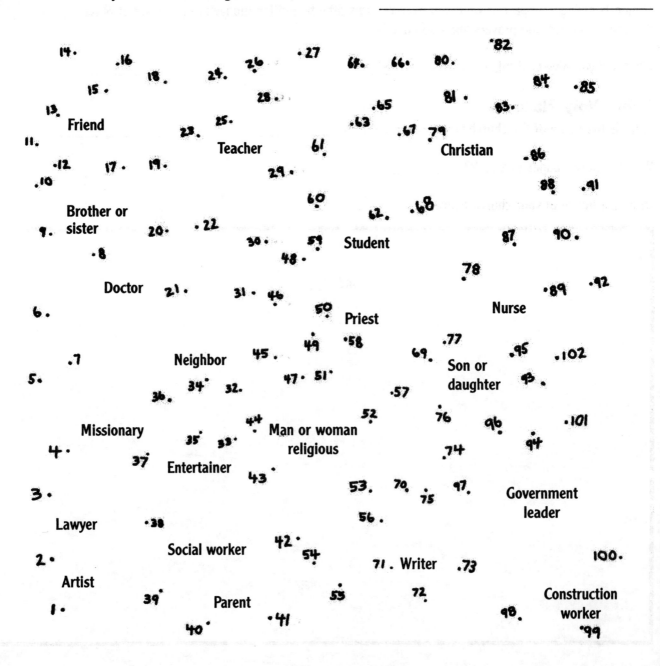

Elijah and the Angel

1 Kings 19:1–18

Elijah was a prophet, someone who speaks for God. In Israel, Queen Jezabel worshiped a pagan god. She killed the prophets of the true God until only Elijah was left. He fled into the desert. When Elijah came to a broom tree, he sat under it and prayed for God to take his life. Then he fell asleep. An angel touched him and said, "Get up and eat." Elijah saw a hearth cake and a jug of water at his head. He ate and drank and then lay back down. Again the angel touched him and told him to eat and drink or else his journey would be too long. Elijah did as the angel said. He then walked forty days and nights until he came to Mount Horeb. There God spoke to him. Elijah lived until a flaming chariot and flaming horses took him to heaven in a whirlwind.

† Our Daily Bread

Do the math to find names for the food God gives us for strength on life's journey. The first one is done for you.

A B C D E F G H I J K L M N O P Q R S T U V W X Y Z

T __ __   __ __ __ __ __ __ __ __ __
Q+3 L−4 A+4   G−2 Z−5 E−2 A+7 F−5 P+2 F+3 W−4 Y−5

__ __ __ __ __   OF   __ __ __ __ __ __
D−2 O+3 J−5 C−2 I−5   F−5 K+3 O−8 A+4 D+8 X−5

† Elijah's Help

In the picture find and circle the letters in the second word of the puzzle above.

Three Men in a Fiery Furnace

Daniel 3:1–30

The king of Babylon had a golden statue made and ordered everyone to worship it. Those who did not adore his god would be cast into a white-hot furnace. Shadrach, Meshach and Abednego were Jewish rulers in Babylon. Of course, they refused to adore the false god. They were tied up and thrown into the furnace. There they walked about in the fire, singing to God and praying for help. The king's men made the fire even greater. Then an angel of God entered the furnace, drove away the flames and made it feel as though a cool breeze were blowing. The three men praised God. The king saw four men walking about unbound. He called, "Servants of the most high God, come out." They did, and the king saw that they weren't harmed at all. He said, "No other god rescues like this." The king promoted Shadrach, Meshach and Abednego.

† Praising God

In the prayer the three men sang in the furnace they call on all creation to "bless the Lord, praise and exalt him above all forever." Among other things they call

Angels of the Lord . . .
You heavens . . .
Sun and moon . . .
All you winds . . .
Seas and rivers . . .
You dolphins and water creatures . . .
All you birds of the air . . .
Priests of God . . .

On the lines below list some things of nature, animals, places, and people.
Then pray a prayer beginning with the above list and continuing with your own. After each name, pray "Bless the Lord. Praise and exalt him above all forever."

NATURE	ANIMALS	PLACES	PEOPLE
_____	_____	_____	_____
_____	_____	_____	_____
_____	_____	_____	_____
_____	_____	_____	_____
_____	_____	_____	_____
_____	_____	_____	_____
_____	_____	_____	_____

Daniel in the Lions' Den

1 Daniel 6:1–28

Daniel was a supervisor under King Darius. Other government leaders were jealous of Daniel but couldn't accuse him of anything bad. They asked Darius to decree that for thirty days no one should ask a god or man for anything except him, the king. The penalty? To be thrown into a den of lions! As a good Jew, Daniel prayed three times a day to God. The new decree didn't stop him.

The jealous men caught Daniel praying and told the king. Darius tried to save Daniel but couldn't change the law. He said, "May your God save you." Daniel was cast into the den, and a stone was rolled over the entrance. The king couldn't sleep. Early the next morning he went to the den and called to Daniel. Daniel replied that God had sent his angel who closed the lions' mouths. The stone was removed, and Daniel walked out unhurt. Darius then decreed that Daniel's God was to be reverenced and feared throughout the kingdom.

† Daily Prayer

Daniel was faithful to prayer. If you pray at the listed times, or would like to form the habit, color the matching part of the picture. Then draw yourself in the den.

A. Morning
B. Night
C. Before meals
D. After meals
E. At Mass

F. When someone needs help
G. When you need help
H. When something good happens

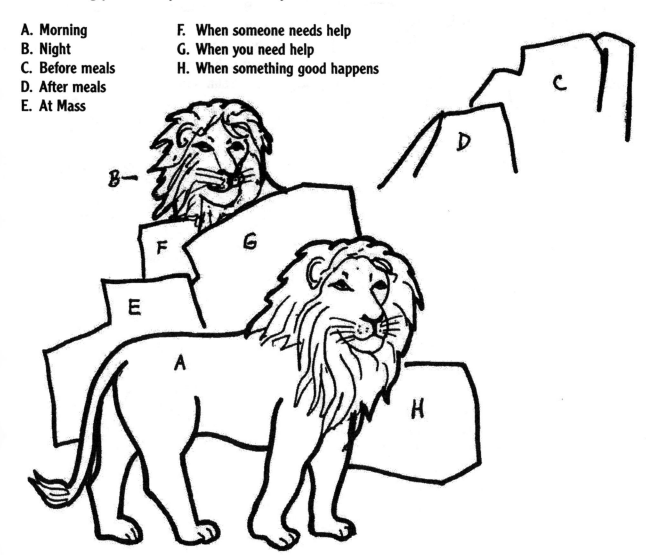

Angels in Psalms

The Bible's 150 psalms are song-prayers. Many are supposedly written by King David, an ancestor of Jesus. Psalms are prayed daily at Mass and in the Prayer of Christians (Divine Office), which is the Church's official prayer. Some psalms mention angels.

† Sing Praise!

Write *angel* or *angels* in the verses where the word belongs. Circle the 8 instruments hidden in the clouds.

You have made them (human beings)
A little lower than the _____.
Psalm 8:5

Bless the Lord,
O you his _____,
you mighty ones who do his bidding,
obedient to his spoken word.
Psalm 35:6

The _____ of the Lord
encamps around those who fear
him and delivers them.
Psalm 34:7

Praise the Lord!
Praise him, all his _____.
Praise him, all his host.
Psalm 146: 1a, 2

For he will command his _____
concerning you to guard you in all your ways.
On their hands they will bear you up,
so that you will not dash your foot
against a stone.
Psalm 91:11–12

St. Joseph, Foster Father of Jesus

Matthew 1:18–24; 2:13-22

Three times St. Joseph received messages from an angel in a dream while he slept. Each time, Joseph followed the angel's directions.

Message One: Marry!

While Joseph was engaged to Mary, she became pregnant. Knowing that he wasn't the father, Joseph was puzzled and decided to quietly break up with her. An angel appeared in a dream and told him to marry Mary. By the Holy Spirit she was going to have a son who would save people from their sins. Joseph was to name him Jesus.

Message Two: Flee!

After Jesus was born and Magi had visited, an angel came and told Joseph to take Jesus and Mary to Egypt. King Herod was going to seek to kill the child. The Holy Family was to stay in Egypt until the angel told Joseph to return.

Message Three: Return!

The angel appeared to Joseph and told him to get up and go back to Israel for the king had died.

† Joseph's Task

Joseph took good care of Jesus and Mary. Now he takes care of something else. Unscramble the letters in the third word below to finish what St. Joseph is patron of.

THE
UNIVERSAL
H H R C U C

_____

† Sent by an Angel

Copy the pieces into their matching places on the grid.

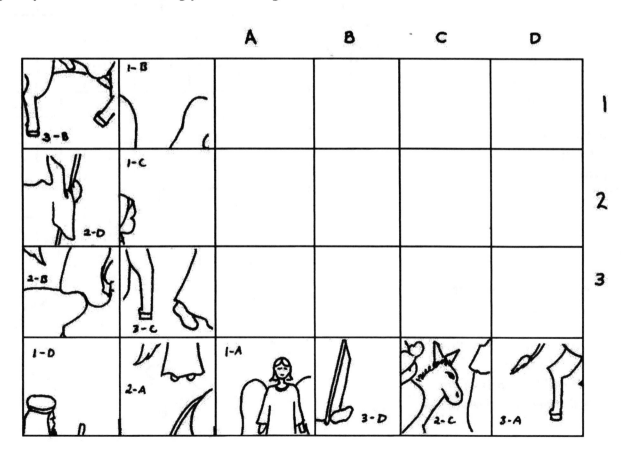

Herald Angels on Christmas

Luke 2:1–20

A herald is someone who announces news. On the first Christmas night an angel appeared to shepherds who were watching their flocks. They were terrified. The angel said, "Do not be afraid; for see — I am bringing you good news of great joy for all the people." (Luke 2:10) He announced that in Bethlehem, the city of David, the savior, the Messiah and Lord, was born. He told the shepherds they would find the child in a manger, an animal feedbox. Suddenly the sky was filled with angels saying, "Glory to God in the highest heaven, and on earth peace among those whom he favors." (Luke 2:14) The angels left, and the shepherds went in a hurry to find the child. When they saw Mary, Joseph and baby Jesus, the shepherds told what they had heard about the child. Then they returned to the fields, praising God for the savior.

† Christmas Crossword

We echo the angels' prayer of praise when we sing or say the Gloria at Mass. Trace the letters to the opening line of this prayer. Then work the puzzle.

> " G L O R Y   T O   G O D
> in the highest and peace to his people on earth."

ACROSS

3. Jesus' birthplace
4. What Jesus is for us
6. Angels told good _____.
7. Herald to shepherds
8. Crib for Jesus
10. The Messiah
11. An announcer
12. Foster father of Jesus

DOWN

1. Day we celebrate Jesus' birth
2. What angels pray people on earth will have
4. The first to hear the Good News
5. Mother of the Savior
9. First word of the angels' praise
12. The feeling the Good News caused

Angels Who Serve Jesus

Three times in the Gospels angels are referred to as serving Jesus. Before Jesus' public life, the Holy Spirit drove him into the desert where he fasted and prayed for forty days. There the devil tempted him, but Jesus did not give in to temptation. Afterward, angels came and waited on him. (Matthew 4:1–11) The night before he died, Jesus prayed in the garden. He dreaded the suffering that was coming but accepted whatever the Father willed. In his agony "an angel from heaven appeared to him and gave him strength." (Luke 22:43) When soldiers came to capture Jesus and an apostle struck one of them, Jesus scolded, "Do you think that I cannot appeal to my Father and he will at once send me more than twelve legions of angels?" (Matthew 26:53) A legion means thousands.

† Prayer of Jesus

Find the prayer Jesus prayed in the garden. Pray it often. Follow the directions to discover each word. Write the entire prayer on the line at the bottom.

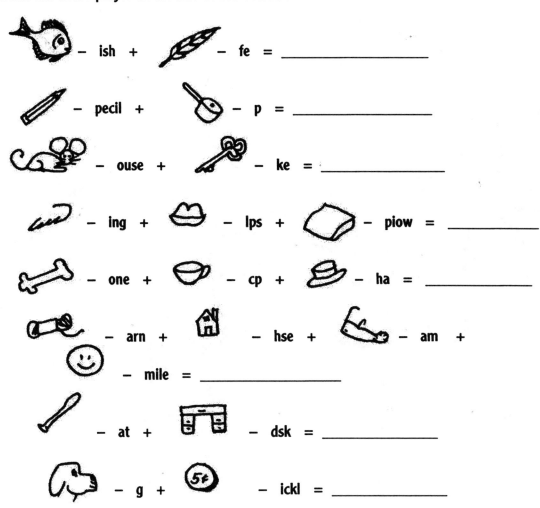

_____

_____

Angels at Jesus' Resurrection

Matthew 28:1-9

Just as angels announced Jesus' birth on Christmas night, an angel announced that he rose from the dead on Easter morning. At dawn there was an earthquake, and an angel rolled back the large stone blocking Jesus' tomb. The Roman soldiers guarding the tomb shook and fainted. When women came to the tomb, they saw the angel sitting on the stone. He was bright as lightning, and his clothes were white as snow. The angel said, "Do not be afraid." He told the women that Jesus was raised as he had said. He had the women look into the empty tomb and then sent them to tell the disciples the good news. On the way, the women met the risen Lord!

† The Easter Scene

Draw the stone the angel sits on. In the word balloon write, "He is risen." Add rays of yellow around the angel. Next to the tomb, draw a lily. Add a butterfly, a symbol of resurrection. On the hill draw three crosses. If you wish, add a fainted soldier.

28

Angels in the Early Church

Acts of the Apostles 5:12-21; 12:1–19

When the apostles taught about Jesus and healed people in his name, Jewish leaders were jealous. They arrested and imprisoned the apostles. During the night an angel opened the prison doors and freed them. He said, "Go, stand in the temple and tell people the whole message about this life."

After King Herod had the apostle James killed, he arrested Peter. The Church prayed for Peter. One night Peter, bound with two chains, was sleeping between two soldiers. Guards were at the door. Suddenly an angel appeared, and light shone in the cell. The angel tapped Peter awake and said, "Get up quickly." The chains fell off Peter's wrists. The angel said, "Fasten your belt and put on your sandals. Wrap your cloak around you and follow me." Peter did as he said. He thought he was seeing a vision. The two passed by the guards and came to an iron gate. It opened by itself, and they went outside and walked along a lane.

The angel left, and Peter realized that the Lord had rescued him. He went to the house where Christians were praying. A maid answered the door. When she announced that it was Peter, the others thought she was crazy. They said, "It is his angel." Then they saw that it was Peter. The next day Herod learned that Peter was missing. He had the guards put to death.

† Apostle Search

Find and circle the names of the twelve apostles in the word search. They are horizontal, vertical and diagonal.

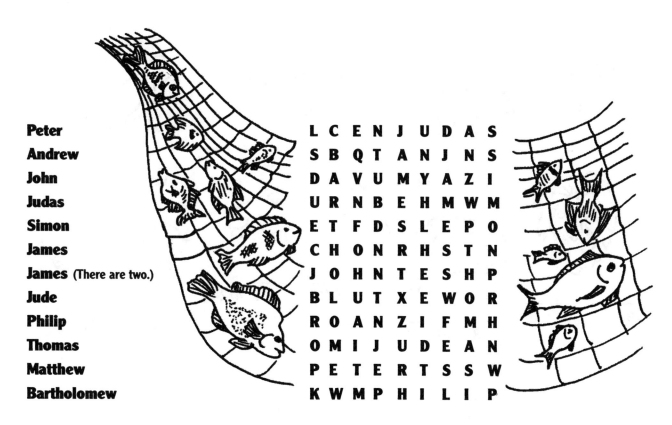

Peter
Andrew
John
Judas
Simon
James
James (There are two.)
Jude
Philip
Thomas
Matthew
Bartholomew

```
L C E N J U D A S
S B Q T A N J N S
D A V U M Y A Z I
U R N B E H M W M
E T F D S L E P O
C H O N R H S T N
J O H N T E S H P
B L U T X E W O R
R O A N Z I F M H
O M I J U D E A N
P E T E R T S S W
K W M P H I L I P
```

Good News for Cornelius

Acts of the Apostles 10:1–48

Cornelius, a Roman army officer, was not Jewish. He was a good man who prayed and gave alms. One day an angel came and called his name. Cornelius stared in terror and asked, "What is it, Lord?" The angel told him to send men to Peter who was in the town of Joppa with a man named Simon. Cornelius sent three men to Joppa. The next day about noon, Peter went on the roof to pray and wait for lunch. He fell into a trance and saw a large sheet come down from heaven filled with all kinds of creatures. A voice told him to kill and eat. Now Jewish laws forbade eating certain animals called unclean. So Peter refused to eat saying, "I have never eaten anything unclean." The voice replied, "What God has made clean, you must not call unclean." This happened three times. Then the sheet rose.

Suddenly the three men arrived and told Peter that an angel had directed Cornelius to send them. In those days Jews did not associate with other people. Peter, though, went to see Cornelius, who had gathered his relatives and friends for the visit. Peter heard Cornelius' story and then told the group about Jesus. Until that time only Jews became Christians. Through the angel and Peter's vision, Peter realized that God's good news was for all people. Everyone in Cornelius's house was baptized that day.

† Animal Hunt

To find the main idea of the story of Cornelius write the name of the animal on the line. Then for each line from 1 to 25 at the bottom of the page put the letter with the matching number.

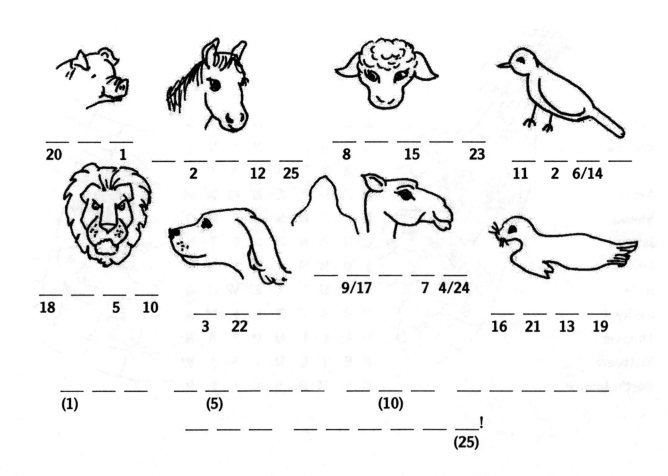

Angels at the End of Time

Matthew 24:30-31

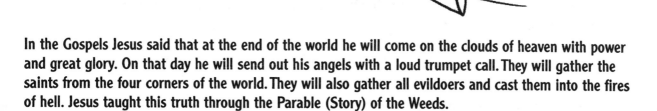

In the Gospels Jesus said that at the end of the world he will come on the clouds of heaven with power and great glory. On that day he will send out his angels with a loud trumpet call. They will gather the saints from the four corners of the world. They will also gather all evildoers and cast them into the fires of hell. Jesus taught this truth through the Parable (Story) of the Weeds.

> ### The Parable of the Weeds
> An enemy sowed weeds in a farmer's wheat field. The farmer let the wheat and weeds grow together until harvest time. Then the weeds were collected and burned and the wheat was stored in his barn. The wheat is like good people and the weeds are like bad people. They live together one earth but at the end of time they will be separated. (Matthew 13:24-30)

Jesus teaches the same lesson in the Parable of the Net. A net catches many fish. When the net is brought in, the good fish are collected and the bad fish are thrown into the fire. (Matthew 13:47–50)

† Weeds and Wheat

Find and circle the 20 dandelions hidden in the wheat field.

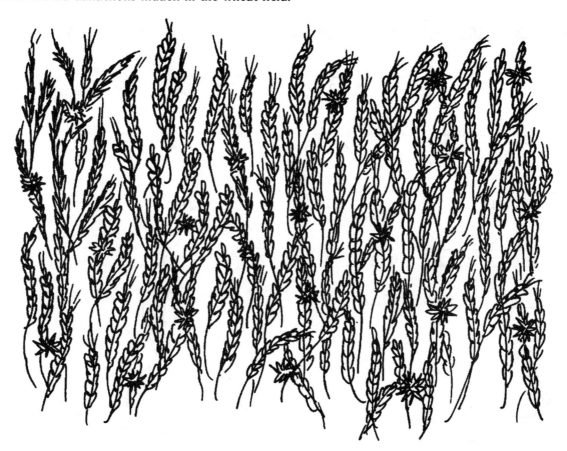

Book of Revelation

The last book of the Bible is the Book of Revelation. It contains the visions that are meant to encourage Christians who were suffering and dying for the faith. In his visions, John saw many angels. They carried out God's commands and spoke to John. At one point John saw angels and many people around God's throne singing a song of praise.

† Glory Song

Use the code to write the words of the song John heard angels and saints singing.

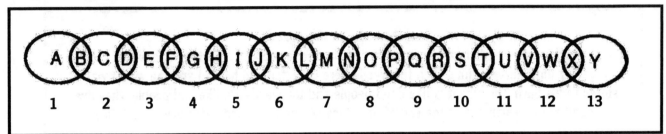

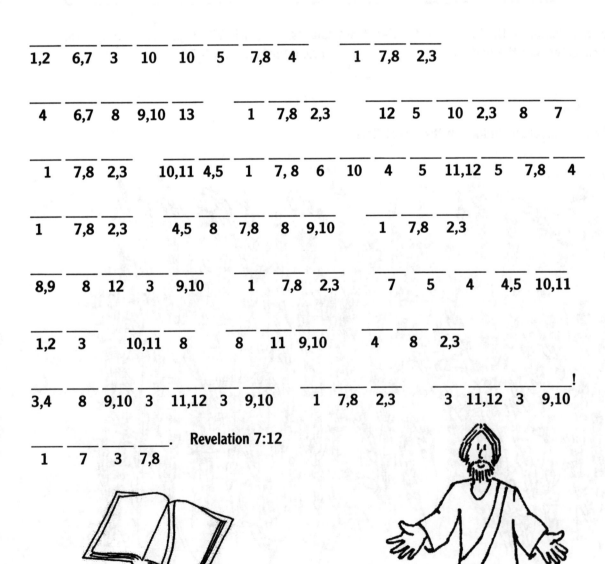

$\dfrac{\text{B}}{1,2}\ \dfrac{\text{L}}{6,7}\ \dfrac{\text{E}}{3}\ \dfrac{\text{S}}{10}\ \dfrac{\text{S}}{10}\ \dfrac{\text{I}}{5}\ \dfrac{\text{N}}{7,8}\ \dfrac{\text{G}}{4}\qquad \dfrac{\text{A}}{1}\ \dfrac{\text{N}}{7,8}\ \dfrac{\text{D}}{2,3}$

$\dfrac{\text{G}}{4}\ \dfrac{\text{L}}{6,7}\ \dfrac{\text{O}}{8}\ \dfrac{\text{R}}{9,10}\ \dfrac{\text{Y}}{13}\qquad \dfrac{\text{A}}{1}\ \dfrac{\text{N}}{7,8}\ \dfrac{\text{D}}{2,3}\qquad \dfrac{\text{W}}{12}\ \dfrac{\text{I}}{5}\ \dfrac{\text{S}}{10}\ \dfrac{\text{D}}{2,3}\ \dfrac{\text{O}}{8}\ \dfrac{\text{M}}{7}$

$\dfrac{\text{A}}{1}\ \dfrac{\text{N}}{7,8}\ \dfrac{\text{D}}{2,3}\qquad \dfrac{\text{T}}{10,11}\ \dfrac{\text{H}}{4,5}\ \dfrac{\text{A}}{1}\ \dfrac{\text{N}}{7,8}\ \dfrac{\text{K}}{6}\ \dfrac{\text{S}}{10}\ \dfrac{\text{G}}{4}\ \dfrac{\text{I}}{5}\ \dfrac{\text{V}}{11,12}\ \dfrac{\text{I}}{5}\ \dfrac{\text{N}}{7,8}\ \dfrac{\text{G}}{4}$

$\dfrac{\text{A}}{1}\ \dfrac{\text{N}}{7,8}\ \dfrac{\text{D}}{2,3}\qquad \dfrac{\text{H}}{4,5}\ \dfrac{\text{O}}{8}\ \dfrac{\text{N}}{7,8}\ \dfrac{\text{O}}{8}\ \dfrac{\text{R}}{9,10}\qquad \dfrac{\text{A}}{1}\ \dfrac{\text{N}}{7,8}\ \dfrac{\text{D}}{2,3}$

$\dfrac{\text{P}}{8,9}\ \dfrac{\text{O}}{8}\ \dfrac{\text{W}}{12}\ \dfrac{\text{E}}{3}\ \dfrac{\text{R}}{9,10}\qquad \dfrac{\text{A}}{1}\ \dfrac{\text{N}}{7,8}\ \dfrac{\text{D}}{2,3}\qquad \dfrac{\text{M}}{7}\ \dfrac{\text{I}}{5}\ \dfrac{\text{G}}{4}\ \dfrac{\text{H}}{4,5}\ \dfrac{\text{T}}{10,11}$

$\dfrac{\text{B}}{1,2}\ \dfrac{\text{E}}{3}\qquad \dfrac{\text{T}}{10,11}\ \dfrac{\text{O}}{8}\qquad \dfrac{\text{O}}{8}\ \dfrac{\text{U}}{11}\ \dfrac{\text{R}}{9,10}\qquad \dfrac{\text{G}}{4}\ \dfrac{\text{O}}{8}\ \dfrac{\text{D}}{2,3}$

$\dfrac{\text{F}}{3,4}\ \dfrac{\text{O}}{8}\ \dfrac{\text{R}}{9,10}\ \dfrac{\text{E}}{3}\ \dfrac{\text{V}}{11,12}\ \dfrac{\text{E}}{3}\ \dfrac{\text{R}}{9,10}\qquad \dfrac{\text{A}}{1}\ \dfrac{\text{N}}{7,8}\ \dfrac{\text{D}}{2,3}\qquad \dfrac{\text{E}}{3}\ \dfrac{\text{V}}{11,12}\ \dfrac{\text{E}}{3}\ \dfrac{\text{R}}{9,10}!$

$\dfrac{\text{A}}{1}\ \dfrac{\text{M}}{7}\ \dfrac{\text{E}}{3}\ \dfrac{\text{N}}{7,8}.$ Revelation 7:12

Escort to Heaven

In a parable that Jesus told, a poor man who dies is carried away to heaven by angels. (Luke 16:19–31) It is a popular belief that when people die, angels take them to heaven. Today at the end of a funeral Mass you might hear the priest pray, "Come to meet him, angels of the Lord! Receive his soul and present him to God the Most High." Or "May the angels lead you into paradise."

Sometimes when a person dies, someone might say, "Now she (or he) is an angel in heaven." That's not true. People are still people in heaven. We don't become angels, but we will have glorified human bodies like the risen Christ has. Also we will be perfectly happy. Why? Because we will see God face to face and be with him, the angels, Mary and the saints forever.

† Maze to Heaven
Find the way from earth to heaven through the maze.

St. Frances of Rome and Her Angel

Frances was born into a noble family in Rome in 1384. Although she wanted to be a nun, Frances married because it was her father's wish. She had three children and managed the family household. Frances always had a large heart for the poor. This led her to open the first home for abandoned children in Rome and also to found a group of women religious who served the poor. Frances endured many hardships including the death of her husband and children. Then she joined the community she founded.

Frances had the grace to see her guardian angel. Other people couldn't see him. He appeared as a 12-year-old boy with blond hair and blue eyes. When Frances ventured out at night to tend the sick and the poor, her angel led the way with a lantern that was like a headlight. She also prayed from her prayer book by the light of the angel. When Frances did something wrong, her angel would tap her hand. When she did penances that were too severe, her angel scolded, "Take care of this body God gave you so that you don't return it ruined." At the end of her life Frances said, "The angel has finished his task. He beckons me to follow him." St. Frances is the patron of widows and motorists. Her feastday is March 9.

† Angel Light
Draw the rest of the picture by copying what is in the opposite square.

St. Catherine Labouré and the Angel

St. Catherine Labouré, a farmer's daughter, was born in 1806. She didn't learn to read because when her mother died, she had to care for the family. At age 14 she joined the Sisters of Charity. Soon after, she began having visions. About 11:30 one night a shining child, probably Catherine's guardian angel, led her to the chapel. There she saw Mary and talked with her for more than two hours. For several months Mary appeared in a picture standing on a globe. Around the picture were the words "O Mary, conceived without sin, pray for us who have recourse to thee." When the picture turned, Catherine saw an M with a cross above it and twelve stars around it. Below were a thorn-crowned heart (the Sacred Heart) and one pierced with a sword (Mary's Immaculate Heart). A voice told Catherine to have a medal cast like the vision. Those who wore it would receive great graces through Mary's prayers.

The priest who heard Catherine's confessions had the medal made. Catherine made him promise not to tell that she was the one Mary had come to. When Catherine died in 1876, people were surprised that such a quiet sister had been favored with Mary's visits. In the convent Catherine had done lowly jobs such as answering the door and caring for the sick and for the poultry! She was canonized in 1947.

† The Miraculous Medal
Connect the dots to complete the two pictures.

 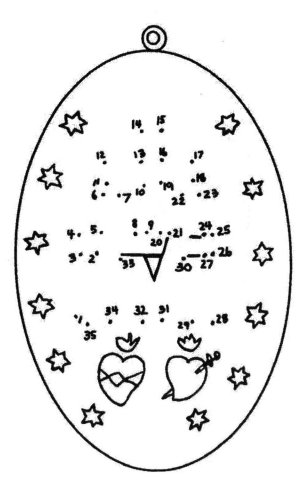

St. Gemma and Her Angel

St. Gemma Galgani (1878–1903) was a beautiful girl who had a difficult life. Her mother died young. Then Gemma had to quit school because of ill health. Her father died, leaving the family in poverty. Gemma became mother to her seven brothers and sisters. Although two men proposed marriage, Gemma wanted to live a life of silence and prayer. When she became very ill and was confined to bed for a year, Gemma accepted her cross patiently. Poor health also kept her from becoming a sister. When she was better, a family took her in. To repay them Gemma did housework and taught their children.

For a time Gemma received the stigmata, the wounds of Jesus in her hands and feet. She also went into ecstasy, a deep prayer where her senses left her. Gemma often saw her guardian angel. He gave her advice, and when she committed a fault he would say, "I am ashamed of you." Gemma talked to her angel as if to a close friend. He is mentioned on almost every page of her diary. Sometimes Gemma sent her angel with messages for her spiritual director. Sometimes a reply came back via his guardian angel. Gemma died of tuberculosis. She was canonized in 1939.

† Sacrifices

In the circle list or draw difficult things that you have to endure. Then pray to your guardian angel to help you to be cheerful in spite of them like St. Gemma. In the box list or draw sacrifices (prayers or good deeds) you will offer to make up for sin. Ask your angel to present your sacrifices to God.

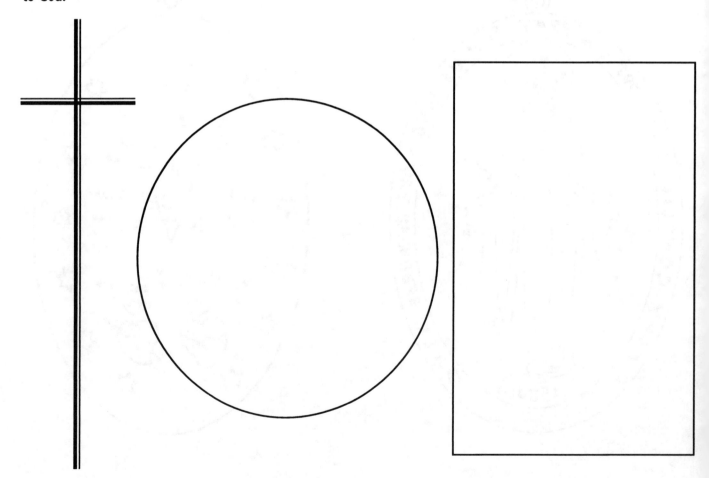

St. Pio of Pietrelcino and Angels

St. Pio, known as Padre Pio, was a Franciscan friar. He was born in Italy in 1887. As a child he wanted to be a priest. He was ordained in 1910. Shortly after Padre Pio's first Mass, while praying before a crucifix, he received a spiritual gift called the stigmata. The bleeding wounds of Jesus appeared on his hands and feet. They would be there for the next 50 years, causing him much pain. Padre Pio treasured the Holy Mass. People flocked to his long Masses and also to his Reconciliation room for confession.

Padre Pio also had the gift of being able to see angels — his own and other people's. He called his angel "the companion of my infancy." People sent their angels to Padre Pio when they needed his prayers. He once remarked about angels, "Do you think they go as slow as planes!" He encouraged a woman to treat her angel not as a friend but as family.

Padre Pio opened a hospital in 1925 and later the House for the Relief of Suffering. He also formed prayer groups. At the age of 81, Padre Pio died. He was canonized in 2002. His feastday is September 23.

† A Good Motto
Find Padre Pio's motto. Color all the pieces that are marked with a star.

QUOTATION *Near us is a celestial spirit who, from the cradle to the tomb does not leave us for an instant.*

The Fatima Angel of Peace

In 1915 while four little girls in Fatima, Portugal, were praying the Rosary, what looked like a cloud with a human outline appeared. This happened twice more. One girl was Lucy. A year later 9-year-old Lucy was tending sheep with her younger cousins Francisco and Jacinta. This time an angel with definite features came and said, "Don't be afraid. I am the Angel of Peace. Pray with me." He knelt, bowed to the ground and prayed, "My God, I believe, I adore, I hope and I love you! I beg pardon of thee for those who do not believe, do not adore, do not hope and do not love thee." The angel told the children to pray this and then left. Another time the angel encouraged them to pray and sacrifice. This would make up for sins, help sinners change their ways and bring peace to Portugal. The angel said he was the guardian angel of Portugal.

Finally the angel appeared holding a chalice and a host. He prayed three times, "Most Holy Trinity, Father, Son and Holy Spirit, I adore thee profoundly and offer thee the most precious body, blood, soul and divinity of Jesus Christ, present in all the tabernacles of the world, in reparation for the outrages, sacrileges, and indifference by which he himself is offended. And, through the infinite merits of his Most Sacred Heart and of the Immaculate Heart of Mary, I beg of thee the conversion of poor sinners." Then the angel gave Communion to the children.

The angel's visits prepared the children for a special visitor. On May 13, 1917, Mary appeared to the children and asked them to pray the Rosary for world peace. She came to them on the thirteenth day of the next six months. Today there is a large shrine at Fatima, and many people have devotion to Our Lady of Fatima.

† The Rosary

Color the Rosary as shown. Then pray it for peace. Begin with the Apostles' Creed. Pray a Glory Be after each set of Hail Marys.

◯	**Our Father** Red
○	**Hail Mary** Blue

Angel Mobile
(Directions are on page 41.)

Honor God's Name.

Obey.

Be pure.

Be honest. Be truthful.

Pray.

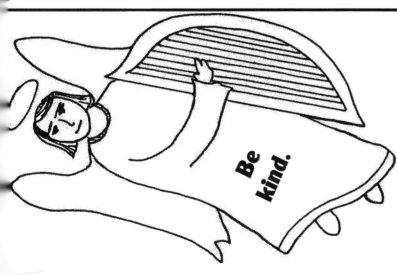

Be kind.

Keep Sunday holy.

Final Angel Activities

Directions for Angel Mobile on page 39

- Color and cut out the angels.
- Cut seven pieces of yarn or ribbon different lengths about 3 to 7 inches.
- Tape one end of each strand to an angel.
- Tie the other end to a clothes hanger.
- Display the mobile where it will remind you of God's Ten Commandments!

† Be an Angel!

Although we never will be angels, we can be like angels by doing holy things, good things. Whenever we do a kind or loving act, we are holier and more like Jesus. We are coming closer to heaven. Has any person ever been like an angel to you? Try for a week to do good deeds. Each night recall what you did. You might draw a pair of wings on a sheet of paper and add a feather for each good deed you do!

Ideas for Angel Acts

Share something. ✦ Compliment someone. ✦ Visit a lonely person. ✦ Do what you're told right away. ✦ Do something without being told. ✦ Clean something. ✦ Help your parents. ✦ When you feel like saying hurtful words, don't. ✦ Give a gift to someone. ✦ Say an extra prayer. ✦ Eat something you don't like. ✦ Say a special thanks to someone. ✦ Give something to the poor.

† Hidden Words

How many words can you make using the letters in ANGEL? Write them here.

_____ _____ _____ _____

_____ _____ _____ _____

_____ _____ _____ _____

_____ _____ _____ _____

_____ _____ _____ _____

_____ _____ _____ _____

Answer Key

Page 1
God, body, think, choose, praise, heaven
Messenger
2, 3, 1, 4

Page 4

Page 5

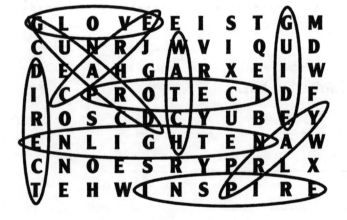

Page 6
Halos for:
 Do what my mother says,
 Share my things,
 Say my morning prayers,
 Participate in Sunday Mass,
 Be kind to someone others avoid,
 Help my mom or dad,
 Do my homework well,
 Clean my room,
 Visit an elderly or sick person,
 Give someone a gift,
 Thank God for good things.

Page 9
Michael, Raphael, Gabriel
Countless

Page 10
evil, live

Page 11
prince, Satan, Who is like God, armor sword,
temptation, lead, scales, Catholic, soldiers

Page 12
Pope Benedict XVI, Rome in Italy or the Vatican, Jesus,
first century

Page 13

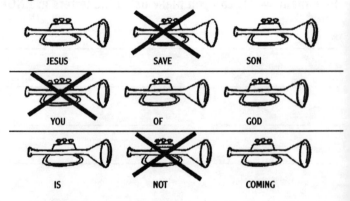

Jesus Son of God is coming.

Page 16
Sacrament of the Anointing of the Sick

Answer Key

Page 17

1. pray, 2. name, 3. holy, 4. obey, 5. kind, 6, 9. pure,
7, 10. Honest, 8. Be truthful

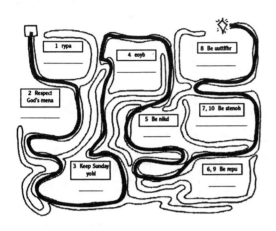

Page 18

Page 21

The Eucharist
Bread of Angels

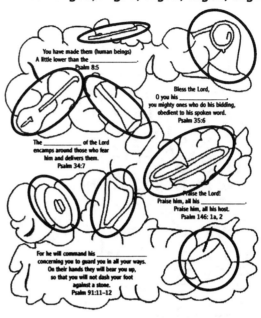

Page 24

Clockwise: angels, angels, angels, angels, angel

Page 25

Church

Page 26

Answer Key

Page 27
Father, not my will but yours be done.

Page 29

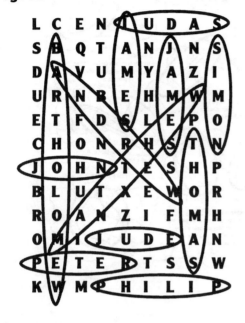

Page 30
Pig, horse, sheep, dove, lion, dog, camel, seal
God loves and saves all people.

Page 31

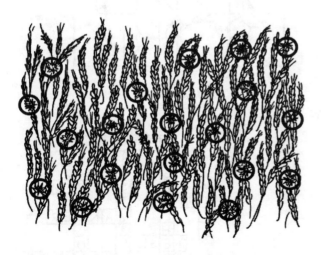

Page 32
Blessing and glory and wisdom and thanksgiving and power and might be to our God forever and ever! Amen.

Page 33

Page 37
Pray, hope, and don't worry.

Page 41
An, as, age, ages, ale, ales, gal, gals, gale, gales, gel, gels, glean, gleans, glen, glens, lane, lanes, lag, lags, lea, leas, lean, leans, leg, legs, lens, sag, sage, sale, sane, sang, sea, sang, snag

44